SAMSUNG GALAXY S22 ULTRA CAMERA USER GUIDE

A Comprehensive User Manual for
Beginners in Mastering   the Latest
Camera Features of Samsung Galaxy
Family, the S22, S22 Plus & S22 Ultra
5G

SANDRA SMITH

Table Of Content

CHAPTER 1 10

  Galaxy S22 Rear Camera Capacity 10

CHAPTER 2 13

  How To Use Galaxy S22 Camera Quick
  Watch? 13

  How To Control Galaxy S22 Camera from
  Galaxy Watch..19

  How To Control 21

CHAPTER 3 24

  How To Take Photo Using S Pen 27

  How To Use Zoom in Features 37

CHAPTER 4 39

  Portrait Mode/ Portrait Video Mode 39

  Pro Mode/Pro Video Mode........................42

  How to Turn on Auto Frame from Video 45

  How to Customize Portrait Shoot 48

CHAPTER 5 50

  Food Mode 50

  How to Use Time Lapse 51

  How to Use Hyperlapse Mode....................51

How to Use the Bokeh Effect Whilst Taking Pictures 52

CHAPTER 6 54

How to Shoot Panoramic Photo 54

How to Superimpose Images 54

How to make Use of the Face Effect 55

CHAPTER 7 58

Super Slow-Motion Mode 58

Motion Videos Automatically How to Record Super Slow 58

CHAPTER 8 61

Video Mode 61

How to Apply Background Music to Video ..62

How To Combine Multiple Video Clips to One 63

CHAPTER 9 66

How To Include Effect to Your Video Calls .66

How To Use This Feature: 67

How To View Video 68

CHAPTER 10 71

Screenshot And Screen Recording 71

How to take a screenshot on the Device 71

How To Enable Shot Suggestion.................76

CHAPTER 11 78

How to Use the Screen Record 78

How To Enable Super Steady Video............81

CHAPTER 12 82

How to Shoot 8k Video..............................82

How to Extract High Resolution Image from a
Footage 84

CHAPTER 13 87

How to modify the Available Camera Modes 87

How to Quickly Switch from Back to Fore
Camera...90

CHAPTER 14 91

How To Enable HDR10 + Shooting 91

In order to use HDR10+ while shooting a
video, you must confirm that you have enabled
it. 91

How To Shoot Raw Images in Galaxy S22 ...92

How to Resize Photos.................................94

CHAPTER 15...97

How to Enable Voice Commands on Galaxy
S22 Camera App 97

How To Use the Auto Frame for Video 99

What Is Samsung Galaxy S22 Voice
Commands 101

CHAPTER 16 103

How To Customize Camera Settings.........103

How to Configure the Shooting Methods ..113

CHAPTER 17 114

How to Create/Decorate an AR Emoji Short
Video 114

How to Activate AR Doodle.....................118

CHAPTER 18 123

Motion and Gesture.................................123

How to Increase the Timer in Night Mode 125

How to Erase Objects from Your Photo 126

CHAPTER 19 128

How to Activate Voice Command.............128

How To Use Smart Select 135

Samsung's Smart Select enables you to select
and crop images without capturing the entire

screen. You can also use it to create GIFs,

extract texts, and pin images. 135

CHAPTER 20 139

How to back up photos and video to one

account 139

How To Reset Camera Settings 140

Tips and Tricks to Improve Photography in

Galaxy S22..144

CONCLUSION 146

INTRODUCTION

Samsung has over the years continued to wax stronger and bigger in the technology sector. As it has evolved significantly bringing innovations and always at the forefront of technology in the mobile device industry and electronic generally.

The Samsung Galaxy S22 series flagship phones come with quite distinctive features such as sophisticated quad camera, S pen, Optical Image Stabilization (OIS), 3x optical zoom, etc.

All the cameras of the Samsung Galaxy S22 does a good job of creating an excellent photography experience for the end user. It can even take good shots at odd hours when the lighting is not so bright.

For unblocking purpose, it come with ultrasonic fingerprint sensor under the display. It also come with Ip68 water/ dust resistance, keeping the phone's inner component free from potential intrusion. It also come with a Gorilla glass victus plus, one of the toughest corning made glasses used in recent times by device manufacturers to shield it from harsh climatic conditions. This feature remains the unbeatable as of the time of its release.

It's offers 5G technology, powered by a 5,000 mAh battery with support for 45w wired fast charging and 15w wireless charging, it has two 10MP telephoto lenses with 3x and 10x optical zooms. This user manual provides you with useful information to be able to perform all possible functions with your camera and take professional pictures, with a lot of tips and tricks to help you become acquainted with the powerful Samsung Galaxy S22, S22 plus and S22 ultra.

In this guide, you' II carefully explores all features and learn to navigate through your Samsung Galaxy S22 camera seamlessly.

CHAPTER 1

Galaxy S22 Rear Camera Capacity

The rear camera of this device is similar to that of the S21 series.

It aids 4k video capturing of up to 60fps and aids capturing of up to 8K locked to 24fps. The 8K view of the S22 is equivalent to the 1x lens. Users who prefer taking videos of almost anything, will definitely love this feature. However, most customers will prefer to utilize the 4K footage since it permits you to zoom in and out, giving you access to all the lenses for 4K capture. The 8K feature is literally there for the purpose of being there and not necessarily for usage.

It comes with three lenses lined up at the rear in one corner. The main lens of the S22 is the

50MP sensor which is more of an improvement to the 12MP sensor that we saw in the previous year. Though it's pixel dims to 12.5MP sensor. We saw that this sensor in particular is enormous than the previous Galaxy S21's 1/1.76-inches. Again, the primary lens comes with an additional 12MP ultrawide camera and a 10MP telephoto lens with 3x optical zoom. The S22 comes with quite distinctive features such as Optical Image Stabilization (OIS), 3x optical zoom, etc.

For selfie lovers, the fore camera has a 10MP hole-punch camera sitting in a cutout on the phone's display with an F2.3 apertures and 1/3.24-inch sensor size.

All the cameras of the Samsung Galaxy S22 does a good job of creating an excellent photography experience for the end user. It

can even take good shots at odd hours when
the lighting is not so bright.

CHAPTER 2

How To Use Galaxy S22 Camera Quick Watch

To make use of the Samsung Galaxy's camera quickly, your best available option would be to use the Galaxy S22 camera quick launch. To achieve this while your phone is locked, press the side key twice.

The side key is on the right side of the Galaxy S22.

This is the fastest approach to launch the Galaxy S22 camera quickly.

The feature is called the Galaxy S22 camera quick launch. It usually works with any Samsung Galaxy phone with One UI or some Android phone like the Pixel phone brand that uses a similar feature.

Note that if you launch the Galaxy S22 Camera Quick Launch without unlocking your device, the phone will limit you from viewing shots from the past other than the new photos taken. This is due to security motives.

The same occurs when you tap the camera app icon on the lock display of the Galaxy S22.

Note that the device quick launch does not operate with flip protections such as the Galaxy S22 LED View Shield. You will need to open the cover in order to use the camera app. You have the benefit, when you are using the Galaxy S22 Smart Clear View (S View). It will ask you to open the shield after you press the side buttons twice before you can take images.

Enabling Or Disabling the Galaxy S22 Camera Quick Launch

By default, you can access the Galaxy S22 camera quick launch in as much as you are through with the initial setup.

If after pressing the side button twice and the camera app fails to open successfully, follow the guidelines below to operate the Galaxy S22 camera quick launch:

☒ Enter the phone's settings

To access this, tap on the Settings icon on the device's home display or go to the Apps display to access the device's settings.

You can also open the Settings icon through the quick settings panel View.

☒ Select Advanced features

Here, you can modify varieties of features on your Galaxy S22.

Since the camera quick launch is a task of the side button, press the Side button, then continue.

⊠ **Explore the Side key customization**

You can customize two signals on this page;

⊠ Double press

⊠ Long press

By default, the double press is set to take you to the Galaxy S22 camera quick launch. You can alter it by tapping on the long press selection.

⊠ **Enable or disable the phone's camera quick launch**

If you formerly designate the double press gesture to open the Samsung Pay or other apps, you can choose the Quick launch camera.

To disable the camera quick launch, modify your choice to Samsung Pay or any apps installed on your device.

To restrict the double press gesture, tap on the switch located on the principal side of the option.

☒ Test the Galaxy S22 camera quick launch

After allowing the camera quick launch, you can go further to test it by double clicking the side button.

Importantly, you can also access the Side key customization side from the Galaxy S22 power-off menu.

You can also use the Side key customization page by selecting the Side key settings.

Limitations of the Galaxy S22 Camera Quick Launch

As stated earlier, you can only consent to one function of the double press gesture of the side key. You have three (3) options, to select from:

1. Camera quick launch
2. Open any other apps installed on the Galaxy S22
3. Pay with Samsung Pay

You will be asked to select one of the aforementioned options. If you want to access the double press gesture to launch the camera of the Galaxy S22, then the other two options will not be enabled.

Samsung Galaxy S22 users who use Samsung Pay always have a way to still make use of it.

You can customize Samsung Pay as the default NFC contactless pay. With this, you can launch the camera app with the side key and also make use of the Samsung Pay.

How To Control Galaxy S22 Camera from Galaxy Watch

Your Samsung smart watch can assist you with many things such as checking time and sending SMS. It can also modify your phone's camera and view whatever your phone display is displaying at that instant. The Galaxy Watch is intended to assist you go about your day-to-day undertakings and perform chores effortlessly.

Whenever your Galaxy S22 is a distance from you (probably on a tripod), you will still be able to take a picture of yourself. It can also demonstrate to be valuable when you're taking a group photograph, as it will enable you to see the image first before capturing it. You will be able to see whatever your device is capturing on the watch's display. You can even tap wherever on the frame to emphasis more on a precise object in the picture.

While you can use the Galaxy Watch to operate your Galaxy S22 camera, you can also enable Samsung Pay, Google Maps, and lots more.

Operators will be able to use this app once they have their Galaxy Watch because the Camera controller app is most times pre-installed. The next phase would be to consent to the different permissions.

On your Galaxy S22, you will be asked to install the app in order for the feature to work.

How To Control

Open the Camera controller app on the Galaxy Watch. This will spontaneously launch the camera of your Galaxy S22.

Before you can be able to capture a decent selfie on your Galaxy S22 with your Galaxy S22, ensure the software is up to date on your Galaxy Watch.

- Tap on the Galaxy Store icon on the Galaxy Watch
- Click on the Search option
- Explore Camera Controller in the search space
- Tap on Camera Controller when found, and choose Install to install the app on your Galaxy Watch

- ☒ Tick to agree to permissions of the Camera controller app

- ☒ Select OK to proceed

- ☒ Proceed to and launch the Camera Controller app on your Galaxy Watch

- ☒ The camera app on your Galaxy S22 will eventually open, then choose your desired camera mode and customize your device to capture the moment

- ☒ Click on the camera shutter key on your Galaxy Watch to take an image on your Galaxy S22

- ☒ Select the thumbnail to view the image on your Galaxy Watch. You can find this image in the Gallery app of your Galaxy Watch and your Galaxy S22

- ☒ Go back to the camera by selecting the back key

☒ You can initiate a delay to the shutter by clicking on the timer icon on the Galaxy Watch

☒ If you want to take a video, switch to Video view on your Galaxy S22 and use your Galaxy Watch to initiate and end the video footage.

Note: The Camera Controller app is enabled on the Galaxy Watch Active, Galaxy Watch Active2, Galaxy Watch3, and Galaxy Watch4.

CHAPTER 3

How To Shoot a Photo

The Samsung Galaxy family, the S22, S22 Plus, and S22 Ultra all have same camera app capability, though the S22 Ultra has improved hardware.

To shoot a photo, you must first enable the camera app. Here are the four ways to initiate the device camera app:

- ☒ Select the Camera image on the home display or Apps display to initiate the Galaxy S22 Camera app

By factory setting, after the successful initial setup of the Galaxy S22, you can find the camera app in the device's home display and App display.

Tap it to initiate your device camera app.

☒ Slide the camera app image on the lock display of the device to initiate the camera app

You can enable the device's camera before getting access to the phone, though you will only be able to view browser photos and videos shot the present session.

By default, there are two app symbols (app shortcuts) on your device lock screen. One on the left extreme of the screen, and the other on the opposite extreme. By factory settings, the device camera app symbol is positioned on the right extreme of the display. To enable it, swipe in any path to the center of the screen. The camera app will launch after performing that.

☒ Make use of your device Camera quick launch by pressing the edge button twice.

This is the quickest means to gain access to the Galaxy S22's camera app. It operates even when the display is off. It will wake the screen up as it initiates the camera app.

☒ Use voice orders like Bixby or Google Assistant to start the device's camera app or take images directly

You can make use of these voice orders at the same time subject to your choices.

You can say "OK, Google, open the Camera app", and it opens it without delay, or say "Take a photo" to make use of the camera app and take a photo, immediately.

Galaxy S22 Camera Interface

According to factory settings, the camera app of this device is usually in the Photo style. You can modify the camera settings to make the camera app opens with the camera mode previously in operation.

The Photos mode of the Galaxy S22 is always in the Auto manner which modify lighting and items present in the preview screen. When you alter it to other camera styles, you may notice a modification in interface.

How To Take Photo Using S Pen

The S pen can simply be the preferred accessories of this device users. It doesn't only enable you to go through your phone, look through pictures in the Samsung Galaxy app, initiate/end video recordings, or preview links or warnings with the S pen, but also enables you to capture shots and footage.

The S pen can also operate as a remote regulator when taking shots. To take a shot, click on the key, which functions as the shutter. It also assists gestures for changing from fore to rear cameras, substituting camera modes, and zooming in and out.

With the aid of this device's S pen, you don't have to run back into the frame after setting the timer. With this S pen, you can confidently take pictures from where you are.

The S pen is most times linked to the Galaxy S22 through Bluetooth and can operate as a remote-control camera trigger from a distance of 10m.

How To Use the S Pen as A Remote Control

Enable the S pen remote control

To ensure this feature operate on the S pen, you will first of all, have to enable it in the settings of your Galaxy S22.

To be able to access this feature to take photos from a far place, follow the guidelines below:

1. Initiate the Settings app on your Galaxy S22

2. Select Advanced features > S Pen

3. Select on Air actions and shift on the toggle in the next screen

Air actions are actions that enable you control aided apps remotely making use of your S Pen.

Note: You can access the Samsung S Pen Air actions in the S pen settings through the S pen itself.

When you eliminate the S pen from your device, the Air Command menu inevitably pops up. click on the Settings icon situated on the lower left angle of the display. Proceed to the Air actions and enable it.

Another method to go about this is by swiping down twice (top bottom) to launch Quick panel. Search for S Pen Air actions alternative, and click on it to enable.

4. Open the camera app on your device.

5. Get rid of the S pen from your smartphone

6. Place your device in the location where you do prefer for the shot to be taken

7. Tap the S pen key once to snap a shot

Once you have effectively taken a photo, you will hear a capture sound.

You can proceed and take more snaps by tapping the S Pen button. If you decide to take a footage, go to video mode and capture a video.

8. Double press the S pen key to shift it, from the front to rear cameras

Note: The S pen may disengage from the Galaxy S22 if it has been detached or have been inactive for a while. If this occurs, re-insert the S pen into the device and permit it to reconnect.

To access the S Pen, first you have to ensure the Air actions feature on your smartphone.

Some S Pen Air Actions in the Camera App

The Air Actions on your smartphone ensure things are easier for users.

Some S Pen Air Activity in the camera app, include;

1. Open the camera app making use of the S Pen

If you choose to speedily open your camera app from whatever display you're on, long press the S Pen key for few seconds.

If this doesn't work, proceed to the Settings app. Select Advanced features, and click on S Pen > Air Actions. Click on Hold down Pen button, and click on Camera.

2. Switch between both cameras

If you decide to switch between the fore and rear camera, click the S Pen button twice in the Camera app.

You can also alter between taking selfies and regular styles by long pressing the S Pen key and moving the S Pen either up or down.

3. Several photos

To take several photos, hold down the S Pen key while making use of the Camera app.

4. Alter shooting modes

While making use of the camera app, you can alternate between diverse camera styles like single take, portrait, etc. Achieve this by long pressing on the S Pen key and switching sideways.

To record a new footage or capture a picture using another mode, click the S Pen button once.

5. Drag in and out in the Camera app

Long tap the S Pen button and revolve clockwise to drag in while using the camera app. Keep your thumb held down on the S pen till you reach your preferred zoom level. Likewise, long hold the S Pen key and revolve anticlockwise to zoom out in the viewfinder.

6. View existing gestures and schedules

Make use of the S Pen to view the existing features and actions that can be applied on the Camera app.

- ☒ Take away your S Pen from your Galaxy S22 to jolt the Air Command menu.

- ☒ Initiate the Camera app and select the floating blue Air Command icon. Select Camera located beside the S Pen's battery

☒ All the existing features and commands for the Camera app will appear.

You will also find the aided features and commands for other apps. To access this, click on the app in place of Camera in the Air Command name.

7. Alter Air Commands set for Camera app

Some operator may not prefer the default settings that commands the features and commands in the camera app. The good side is that you can effortlessly change it to your preferred choice.

If the default gesture for alternating between cameras is the single press command, you can choose to alter it in the Settings app.

Go to Settings, select Advanced Features > S Pen > Air Actions. Tap the Camera app under the App actions.

You can alter the default settings and actions here. You can entirely disable the actions with the toggle at the top.

To personalize an action, pick the action and pick a fresh method from the menu bar.

8. Look through photos from the app

Though this comes after taking pictures, it might also be convenient to users.

Customers can go through their gallery app in their Galaxy S22 with their S Pen.

When you select a picture, tap the S Pen key once to move to the succeeding or double tap the S Pen to go to the previous photo.

Applying Filter and Beauty Effects

What are filters and beauty effects?

Filters and beauty effects is a feature on the device that lets you pick a filter effect and augment your facial tone or structure beforehand.

You can add a camera filter and beauty effects to a photo after saving it.

While you can add effects while editing them, some operator would decide to use the face filter while taking a picture to enhance their skin.

Guidelines to apply filter and beauty effects on the device;

- ☒ Open the camera app on your device
- ☒ On the preview display, pick the Filters and Effects icon
- ☒ Select a filter from the options and take a shot

How To Use Zoom in Features

Galaxy S22 aids hybrid optical and super-resolution zoom.

On default, four pre-set zoom ranks are present on the Galaxy S22 Ultra; 0.6x, 1x, 3x, and 10x.

Pick any of the four icons to select a zoom rank. Once you tap any of the four icons, more pre-set zoom stages up to 100x will pop up (usually present in the Galaxy S22 Ultra).

If you zoom in the preview screen, additional slider is included, where you can better regulate the zoom.

CHAPTER 4

Portrait Mode/ Portrait Video Mode

Portrait Mode

There are diverse camera modes on the device. These camera modes are pre-set configurations for the device camera.

The portrait mode is a new addition of the device camera. Both the fore and rear cameras, can be put to use.

In the portrait style, the Galaxy S22 assumes configurations to the camera by obscuring the background (bokeh effects) and tweaking the color brilliance and contrast for the user.

The Galaxy S22 camera modes were specially aimed to provide the preferred pictures and footages made for distinctive instances without having to do so in the settings.

In other words, the device portrait style takes shots with a modifiable depth of focus. You can alter the bokeh effects on the Gallery App if the portrait style was used to take the picture.

You can also choose diverse bokeh effects when taking the photo.

Portrait Video Mode

The enhanced portrait video mode is a very obvious features of the device.

With portrait mode, you can use beauty special effects and filters to beautify your selfies.

The portrait video style on the hand is similar to Live Focus, but you can improve the effects and filters to improve your pictures. Just like in the portrait mode where you can add special effects to your photos, the portrait video mode assists to add effects and filters to what you're recording; either using the fore or rear cameras.

Likened to the Portrait style, the device's portrait video mode doesn't have studio and backdrop effects.

How to use:

- ☒ Select the Camera app of your Galaxy S22

- ☒ Open More

- ☒ Pick Live focus video or Portrait video

- ☒ Click on the circle placed at the foot right of the viewfinder. Select from the four options that will be shown. You can resolve to alter any making use of the slider.

- ☒ Big circle: This creates a focused circle round the involved object, then blurs out the other parts of the background.

- ☒ Blur: This aids to blur out the background around the object you're filming.

- ☒ Color point: This alters the brightness of the colors that surround the concerned subject, so that the background is shown in dark and grey.

- ☒ Glitch: This will aid a colorful static effect in the background.

Pro Mode/Pro Video Mode

Pro mode

The Galaxy S22 Pro mode is a property for operators who are interested in photography and accepts several adjustments.

The Pro mode permits you to change specific areas of the photography; allowing you to alter the shutter rate, auto focus, ISO, exposure, and many other photographic adjustments that you desire.

Users can save the photos that have been taken in the Pro mode in the RAW form (in addition to the normal JPEG or HEIF format). This aids you to further process it in any specialized photography app of your choice you desire.

Pro Video Mode

The Pro video mode is the video version of the Pro mode in the device.

Likened to the Pro mode in the Galaxy S22, the Pro video mode offers you many photography settings to pick from whole filming; you can alter the shutter speed, zoom level, ISO, auto focus, and many other photographic adjustments.

Some users go for the Pro video approach for the sake of, flexible audio input bases. Some of the different audio inputs available for users to choose from:

- ☒ Front: This aid the sound coming from the object in focus to be shot while the sound from the rear (camera man side) will be subdued.

- ☒ Rear: The direct opposite of the fore. Sound coming from the back side will be captured, while sound coming from the front will be muffled.

- ☒ Omni: Audios coming from all directions will be noticed.

- ☒ USB: The audio input created by the USB source will be noticed.

☒ Bluetooth: The audio input coming from the Bluetooth mic will be noticed.

☒ BT mix: This allows you to blend the mic input from a Bluetooth headset (e.g Galaxy Buds Live) with others.

How to Turn on Auto Frame from Video

☒ Select the Camera app

☒ Click on Video mode

☒ Tap Frame to support it

☒ Pick the frame round the subject to track and alter the shooting viewpoint and zoom in on the subject.

☒ To disable tracking, pick the frame again.

Video Brightness

☒ Select the Camera app

☒ Tap on Video

☒ Click the screen to display the brightness icon presented by a lock

☒ A bar with a small sun image will be shown below the lock icon. Slide it to the left or right to change the brightness

☒ Tap the Record icon to initiate recording

☒ Tap the Stop icon to end recording. The video will appear spontaneously in the Gallery app after it has been saved.

Video Enhancer

Samsung changed the Video Enhancer to Video Brightness on the device, which is preferably appropriate for this property.

This property makes your screen brighter and makes the colors appear more effervescent while you're watching videos. This will let you from manually changing your device brightness every time you watch a video. It is also accessible on every app.

How to enable Video Enhancer:

- ☒ Open the Settings app
- ☒ Pick Advanced Features and click on it
- ☒ Select Video Enhancer or Video Brightness
- ☒ Tap on the Bright option on the right side

☒ You can now pick the app that you desire to use Video Enhancer in. By default, it enhances most video apps on Android.

How to Customize Portrait Shoot

☒ Open the Camera app, select Portrait. To add special effects before capturing the photo, tap Portrait Effects at the lower right of the display

☒ Pick any of the shown options; Blur, Studio, High-Key Mono, Low-Key Mono, Backdrop, or Color Point. Change the slider from Effects strength below until the filter looks satisfactory to select the Brightness icon on the right part of the viewfinder to modify the brightness

☒ Select Capture when ready

⊠ Click the thumbnail in the lower left corner to display the pictures in the Gallery App. Select the Edit icon to edit the photo if you desire

⊠ There are several editing options to select from. When you're done editing, tap Done

⊠ If you desire to start from the beginning, tap Revert, then click Revert to original

⊠ Click Save to save your new photo, then tap Save again

Note: To keep the original photo, tap the three vertical dots, then tap Save as copy.

CHAPTER 5

Food Mode

The device Food mode permits you to take photos of food by automatically changing the colors of food in the timeframe and obscuring the background to single out the food.

The food mode offers two options for the user when in use;

- ☒ Color temperature: This property automatically changes the color temperature of a photo when used.

  You might decide to change this feature with the default settings.

- ☒ Radial blur: The Galaxy S22 Food mode adds a radial blur to the timeframe to highlight the food in question. According to factory settings, the emphasis of the feature is at the midpoint. You can modify the size and the position of the area in focus.

How to Use Time Lapse

To make use of the Galaxy Time Lapse,

- ☒ Select the Camera app
- ☒ In the rear camera, adjust to Hyperlapse
- ☒ Click on the screen to start recording
- ☒ Tap to stop the time-lapse video.

How to Use Hyperlapse Mode

The Hyperlapse mode was first presented in the Galaxy S7. However, some modifications have been made over times for this camera mode.

Galaxy S22 Hyperlapse mode let you to produce your own time-lapse video.

The camera mode lets you to record the scene at diverse frame rates (time-lapse speed). It can automatically change them to produce amazing time-lapse videos.

You can select the resolution as either FHD or UHD.

How to Use the Bokeh Effect Whilst Taking Pictures

To make use of the Bokeh effect on your Smart device, you will need to use a mode which is by default to cover the background. This is the mode that will be supported when you take the snapshot.

☒ Tap on the Camera app

☒ Select the Live Focus mode

☒ Change the blur intensity using the adjustment bar

☒ Capture your snapshot when you have reached the desired blur effect.

CHAPTER 6

How to Shoot Panoramic Photo

This Smartphone, panorama mode allows up to 360° scenes into one panorama photo.

While you're in the panorama mode, an adjustment box will be made accessible to help you keep the scene aligned.

You can now shift the device slowly in a specific direction.

How to Superimpose Images

- ☒ Open the Gallery app, and select any image you desire.
- ☒ Select the Edit image at the lower right of the display screen

- Tap the Sticker icon and pick the Gallery tool at the foot right.

- Select another image from the Gallery app that you desire to add to the original photo

- Select the photo and resize it if you desire, dragging the handles.

- select the Save button at the upper part of the screen.

How to make Use of the Face Effect

The Face Effect option permits you to eliminate red-eye, brighten your skin tone, and even make your eyes seem bigger.

Note: The Face Effect only appear while modifying photos of people or selfies.

- Open the Gallery app and select the photo you intend to edit

☒ Select the Edit icon and tap More options, then select Face effects.

☒ Choose the desired editing options; Tone, Red-eye fix, and Smoothness.

☒ After making your selection, follow the displayed guidelines or modify the slider to select your desired intensity For instance, the Spot fixer eliminates blemishes from the face by tapping on the portions of a person's face.

☒ Tap Done when you're done editing Note: Use the arrows to undo or redo your editing if you commit any error.

☒ If you intend to start over, tap on Revert, then tap Revert to original

☒ To save your edited picture, tap Save, then tap Save again

Note: You can save the original photo by tapping on More options, then tapping Save as copy.

CHAPTER 7

Super Slow-Motion Mode

The Super slow-motion mode was introduced in the Galaxy a few years back, and it has been slightly upgraded since then.

On this device S22, the super slow-motion mode permits you to record a 720p video at 960fps for up to 1 second.

Motion Videos Automatically How to Record Super Slow

The improved speed sensor on the device, Super Slow-motion lets you to shoot at an astonishing speed of 960 frames per second.

Super Slow-motion mode only aids HD resolution, and is restricted to 20 slots per video.

The best technique to enjoy the Super Slow-motion is to make use of the Auto mode. Here, the camera will automatically notice motion and slow it down. It also permits you to add a slow-motion action as you desire in a specific video.

☒ Open the Camera app

☒ Select More, then tap on Super Slow-motion

☒ Enable the auto mode by tapping on the Motion Detection image. It will be displayed as three small balls in a square

☒ Select Record when ready. Hold your device fixed to begin motion detection

☒   Once the Camera senses any reaction in the square, it automatically begins recording.

Slow Motion Style

The device slow-motion mode permits you to record full HD (1080p) videos at 240fps.

You cannot change the resolution or frame rate of the camera mode.

If you prefer to use a greater frame rate, you can fully enjoy that in the super slow-motion feature which records HD (720p) videos at 960fps in 1 second.

CHAPTER 8

Video Mode

Galaxy S22 Video mode is the default camera mode that the device permit to record videos in the Camera app.

It is the video form of the Photo mode for pictures.

Some modified settings will be added automatically to the videos recorded.

When you make use of the fore camera to record a video on the device, you can decide to pick the mirrored or the non-mirrored video in the device camera settings.

How to Apply Background Music to Video

After shooting a video or a video is sent to you, at times we may desire to edit the video in the video editing app to better suit our taste. You can make use of the footage editing app in either portrait or landscape feature to edit videos, no matter the method you shot the original video.

Follow the guidelines below to add background music to your videos:

- ☒ Open the Samsung Gallery app and pick the video which you would like to edit

- ☒ Select the pencil icon found at the bottom left of the screen, and it will take you to Samsung video editor

- ☒ You can now decide to include music, transitions, and text to the preferred video

- ☒ After editing, select the save key to make your file visible subsequent timeworn you need it.

How To Combine Multiple Video Clips to One

On this device, you can easily include different video clips of your choice into one video. Two methods can be Selected to combine different videos into one on this device. The first method includes:

- ☒ Open the Samsung Gallery app, pick the video you'd desire to edit

- Click on the film icon in the top right corner and pick the files you wish to edit
- Select Create Movie at the foot of the display, and click on Edit yourself to initiate the procedure
- Click on the pencil icon beneath the screen at the left-hand side, and you'll be directed to the Samsung video editor
- Here, you can input music, transitions and others to the movie scenes
- Save the video for future purpose

The other method of combining different videos into one includes:

- Enter the Gallery app, pick any of the videos you'd prefer to merge

- Select the edit button in the lower left of the display (it will be displayed as a pencil)
- Tap Add at the top of the display and pick the second video you would prefer to combine.
- Select different videos and images if you desire, and tap Done
- A new timeline for the just created video appears at the lower part of the screen. Select transition markers between video clips to add to the transition or leave the default by opting for a clean cut
- Click on Save at the top of the screen to save your new video.

CHAPTER 9

How To Include Effect to Your Video Calls

Galaxy S22 lets users to include background effects to their video calls.

This property is usually used to alter the background colors, blur effect, and pictures. The Samsung video call effect also subdue background sound that may be heard while on video calls.

Follow the guidelines below to enable this feature and alter the video background in video call apps.

- ☒ Enter the Galaxy Settings app
- ☒ Navigate to the Advanced Features
- ☒ Click on Video call effect
- ☒ Select the toggle by its side to allow it

⊠ A video call icon will be shown in the video calling app's screen

How To Use This Feature:

⊠ Pick the video call icon on the video calling screen, and pick any of the choices that appear.

⊠ Reset all: Reset the existing settings

⊠ Background: Edit or blur the background during video calls

⊠ Auto framing: You can decider allow or disallow this feature. When you allow it, the device shifts from its original shooting viewpoint and automatically zooms into any person on the screen during video calls.

⊠ Mic mode: Subdue any noise coming from the video's background to make the sound flawless

☒ Standard: Mute the noise, so that it functions as a typical video call

☒ Voice focus: This option enables you to specially filter the noises from the front camera

☒ All sound: Enables the sound that can be heard around you such as the sound of music

☒ Settings: Include background colors or images during video calls.

How To View Video

When you select the Galaxy S22's phone gallery, you will see pictures and video clips taken with the device camera or video recorder.

☒ Enter the Gallery app, and scroll to the desired folder where the specific video was saved

☒ Select the specific video, and you can now view it

☒ Go back to the home display by tapping on the home key.

Viewing Brighter and Clearer Video

The device's Vision Booster is a stand-out property that modifies the screen's brightness under direct sunlight to enhance image visibility.

The vision booster is crucial because a surge in the max out brilliance of white is not sufficient to let a picture or video clear. The modifications of midzones and shadows in moderate proportions will make the screen brighter and clearer under sunlight.

CHAPTER 10

Screenshot And Screen Recording

The Galaxy S22 has comparable methods of taking screenshots and screen recordings as other One UI devices. There are methods that Galaxy S22 users can take screenshots and screen recordings and select alternatives to screenshot and screen record.

How to take a screenshot on the Device

The easiest way is to hold down on the volume and power buttons simultaneously. This will capture an image on the device display.

There are other methods to take a screenshot:

1. Touch gesture: To check if the touch gesture is allowed, go to the Settings app and search for Palm swipe. This feature enables you to swipe your thumb from the end of the display towards the left or right of the display to take a screenshot.

2. Google assistant: Once the Google assistant is enabled, say "Ok Google, take a screenshot" to take a screenshot. The same method works for Samsung's Bixby. Say "Hey Bixby, take a screenshot" to capture it.

Whenever you use any of the ways aforementioned, a toolbar will appear at the end of the screen with more options.

The downward-facing arrow button enables you to scroll to make a lengthier screenshot. The share button let you to share this screenshot to any app that permits you to import images. The hashtag button permits you to tag the screenshot for better documentation. The crop button permits you to crop the screenshot at that instance.

3. S pen: When you remove the S pen out of your Galaxy S22, click on Smart select in the menu that pops up. Then, draw an outline of the area you intend to capture. It will save as a screenshot.

Screenshot On Samsung Dex

This device series have a feature called the Samsung DeX that lets users to view their phone's apps on a multi-window, similar to a typical desktop mode.

While in the Samsung DeX, users can take screenshots through a dedicated screenshot button at the right-hand side of the task bar. This is because the screenshot methods aforementioned don't work on the Samsung DeX.

Press the screenshot button at the right-hand side of the screen(taskbar) or hold down or right-click the screenshot button to take a half screenshot.

Screen Recording on The Galaxy S22

There are quite a few methods to screen record on the Galaxy S22 compared to the options available for capturing screenshots.

The first option is to tap on the Screen recorder option in the quick settings panel. You can locate it in the same area as the Bluetooth and Wi-Fi toggles.

If it is concealed by default on your device, tap on the three-dot icon at the right-hand side of the top of the screen where the settings panel is situated. Click Edit buttons, and drag the Screen recorder into one of the accessible buttons.

Screen Recording on The Screen Recorder Quick Settings Panel

The device will firstly, inquire if you desire to screen record without sound and media sounds or with sound and your microphone.

Select the desired method and tap Start recording to start the screen record.

The second option that you can use to screen record on the Galaxy S22 is the Samsung Bixby voice assistant. Once it is allowed, say "Hey Bixby, begin a screen recording."

How To Enable Shot Suggestion

Shot suggestions are suggestions to correctly position the direction of your subject while taking shots on the camera app.

How to allow shot suggestions:

- ☒ Search for the Camera app
- ☒ Search for the camera settings
- ☒ Tap on Shot suggestions to allow it

How to make use shot suggestions:

☒ Tap Photo from the list of shooting modes. A pop up of a guide will show on the preview screen.

☒ Direct the guide to the subject. The camera will identify the composition and recommend the accurate composition on the preview screen

☒ Modify your device until the guide suits the suggested composition until the guide changes to yellow

☒ Tap capture to take a photo

CHAPTER 11

How to Use the Screen Record

The screen record mode on the device enables you to take a video of your current screen to share or save for future references.

Screen recording can be put in used for numerous reasons, and the Galaxy S22's extra features like screen drawing and picture-in-picture recording. This allows cutting off other apps since you can simply edit your screen records from your device's Gallery app.

How to screen record:

- ☒ Swipe down twice from the top of the display to view the quick menu

- ☒ In the Quick Settings Menu, click on the Screen Recorder icon in the lower right of the display

⊠ Select any customization you desire, and then proceed to initiate the screen recording. Tap on the Start recording key on the lower right of the display

⊠ A countdown will begin, and your screen recording starts immediately after

⊠ Select any of the Galaxy S22's added options (draw on, pause recording, etc.) in the menu found in the upper right angle of the display

⊠ In order to terminate the recording, pick the square Stop button on the right-hand side.

Capturing An Area from A Video

The Galaxy S22 device can capture areas from a video. Follow the guidelines below to easily capture a portion of footage from your Galaxy S22 device.

- ☒ Open the Gallery app on your Galaxy S22

- ☒ Select on the specific video you would like to work on.

- ☒ Tap on the three dots icon located at the bottom right of the screen

- ☒ Tap Open in Video Player

- ☒ Zoom into the video to choose the preferred frame

- ☒ When you've found the intended frame, tap the Capture frame icon situated at the top left of the screen

- ☒ since you have chosen the frame, tap on the preview window at the bottom

left of your screen to view the
captured frame

☒ You can now view the captured image
on your device Gallery app.

How To Enable Super Steady Video

☒ Enter the Camera app

☒ Select Video on the shooting modes

☒ Tap on Shooting options

☒ Click on Super steady to allow it

☒ Begin recording the video

CHAPTER 12

How to Shoot 8k Video

To shoot an 8K video on your Galaxy S22,
you will need to allow the 8K setting in your
Camera app. You can now begin to trim the

video using the Editor. You can also use the Pro video mode to capture 8K photos.

- ☒ To initiate the video, tap the Camera app on your device

- ☒ Select Video, and pick the Ratio icon and set the resolution to 9:16 8K or 9:21 8K

- ☒ Tap on Record to start filming

- ☒ If you intend to save a high-resolution video while shooting an 8K video, tap on Capture

- ☒ After filming, you can find the video in your Gallery app

- ☒ Tap on Play video, then click on the screen as the video is playing

- ☒ Pick the Gallery icon by the left to take high resolution 33MP pictures of the video

Note: You can find the resolution of the image in your Galaxy S22's Gallery app.

Position the image and swipe up. The anticipated resolution should be 4320×7680.

⊠ For you to edit the video, tap on the three vertical circle, and select Editor

⊠ Cut the video using the slider below the video. Swipe the music icon to edit the video sound or include background music. If more edits are made, it will automatically transform the video to 4K when you save it

⊠ Click Save to save changes made to the footage.

Note: You can modify the resolution of the footage from 8K to any other desired resolution. Click on Resolution and choose any other resolution.

How to Extract High Resolution Image from a Footage

On your device, you can take high resolution still images from footage.

This feature especially comes in suitable for people who can't let go of a certain view in a video.

There are many ways to capture a still image from a footage. After capturing the image, you can modify the image to your heart's content since it is full high-quality resolution.

How to take high resolution image from video through the Gallery app:

- ☒ Initiate the Gallery app on your Galaxy S22

- ☒ Locate the video that you want to remove the image from

- ☒ Play the video and pause it at the point where you intend to capture
- ☒ Tap on the Capture button at the top left of the screen
- ☒ You can preview the screenshot from your Gallery app under Video captures

To take high resolution image from video through PLAY it:

This is another method to capture a still image from a video on your device. PLAYit video player enables users to view videos on their app while retaining the media's quality. The PLAYit video player has so many unbelievable features for users.

Follow the steps below while using the PLAYit app:

- ☒ Open the PLAYit video player and pick the particular video and play it
- ☒ Click on the Scissors icon to make a screenshot
- ☒ You can view the screenshot in your Gallery app under Pictures

CHAPTER 13

How to modify the Available Camera Modes

By default, in most areas, only 3 camera modes are made accessible to Galaxy S22 users above the shutter key.

So, if you intend to use other camera modes, click on the More button to enable the others.

After choosing your desired camera mode, you will be requested to press the Back key to go back to the original interface and access other Galaxy S22's camera modes.

However, it is easier to access when you include all Galaxy S22's camera modes to the default interface to avoid going back and forth.

To edit the Galaxy S22's camera modes, follow the guidelines below:

⊠ Select the camera modes page in the camera app. You can access it in two ways; pick the More option or swipe from right to left. Then, you access the camera modes page.

⊠ In the Galaxy S22's camera app, you will find the existing camera modes above the camera's shutter button. The camera modes found here can only be opened through this page, before they are included to the camera modes bar. Press Back to switch camera modes.

⊠ Pick the plus icon to open the edit mode. By so doing, you are including any of your desired camera modes to the main camera interface.

☒ Once open in the camera mode, double tap any camera mode other than Photo and Video and navigate them.
If you decide to include the Pro mode, double tap the icon and adjust it to your desired location on the camera mode interface.

☒ Now you can see your desired camera mode in the camera mode interface. You can include more camera modes by repeating the procedure.

☒ Save the customization by tapping the Save button to save the modification made.

Now you can view the desired camera mode on the camera mode interface without clicking the More button. You can also control between camera modes without using the

Back key or back gesture if you enabled your navigation gestures.

Note that your device enables you to operate the camera mode buttons without opening your device. This means you can edit your camera modes as long as you launch your camera app. You can initiate it through the camera shortcut or through the Galaxy S22 quick launch.

How to Quickly Switch from Back to Fore Camera

⊠ Open on the Camera app from the home display or swipe up or down from the midpoint of the display to enter the Camera app

⊠   Pick the Camera facing icon to change camera from back to fore camera.

CHAPTER 14

How To Enable HDR10 + Shooting

In order to use HDR10+ while shooting a video, you must confirm that you have enabled it.

⊠   Enter the Camera app

⊠   Click on the Settings icon by the left-hand side at the top of the display

⊠   Pick Advanced recording options under Videos

⊠   Click on the toggle close to HDR10+ to allow it.

How To Shoot Raw Images in Galaxy S22

You can find the Galaxy S22's camera pro mode in the default camera app of the device, however the Expert RAW has an app dedicated solely for it. The app gives you access to more detailed photography and enables you to capture in both RAW and JPEG instantly.

Expert RAW isn't only limited to photo experts, but anyone can use the app to their own advantage. An Expert RAW's picture has all the RAW exposures fit into the photo unlike the usual RAW photos with one frame. The device Expert RAW is closely comparable to the factory settings camera app of the device. However, in the app, the Photo, Video, and Portrait default camera modes will be substituted with more defined settings like

ISO, white balance and shutter speed. You can decide personalize other detailed settings here.

The Expert RAW makes things simpler, and you can go through its settings and pick between automatic and manual style. There is also a reset button to alter everything to the original state if you've made a terrible error with editing.

You can view the photos you've shoot in the Gallery app, mixed in with other images representing the RAW versions and will have a little RAW badge at the top right when viewed in the Gallery app) and in the Expert RAW app, showing you the RAW and JPEG copies of the photos.

Note: In the Expert RAW app, you can't take shots outside the 4:3, shots, portraits, or selfies.

Guidelines on how to shoot RAW photos on your device

- ☒ Enter the Camera app on your device

- ☒ Select the Settings icon at the top left of the display

- ☒ Navigate to Format and pick Advanced options

- ☒ Pick the toggle next to RAW copies to switch it on

The device will normally save RAW copies when whooping in the Pro camera mode which you can access from the More option found in the bottom of the Camera app.

How to Resize Photos

You can modify the size of a photo after the shot using the Camera app. The photo editor in the Gallery app is the suitable place to resize your photos in the Galaxy S22.

Note: Before following the guidelines below, ensure your phone's software's and related apps is updated.

Follow the guidelines below to resize a photo on the Galaxy S22:

- ☒ Open the Gallery app and pick the image you desire to resize

- ☒ Pick the Edit icon found at the bottom of the display

- ☒ Tap on the three vertical dots at the top right to show more options

- ☒ Pick Resize

- ☒ Select your desired resized image percentage from the Resize percentage options, and click on Done to make changes

- ☒ Click Save to save the changes made to the Image

Having effectively resized the photo, and you can view the resize information's of the image file

CHAPTER 15

How to Enable Voice Commands on Galaxy S22 Camera App

It was in the Galaxy S7 series that Samsung initiated camera voice controls.

Here are some methods you can follow to take a shot or shoot a video by simply using static commands or phrases.

After allowing this feature, you can capture photos by saying Cheese, Capture, Shoot, or Smile.

To shoot Footage, you can say Record video, and your phone immediately starts to record.

This is all thanks to Samsung's virtual mobile assistant known as S Voice.

This recent improvement saves time and effort that you would have normally used in going through the menu.

Guidelines on how to enable voice commands on your device

- ☒ Enter the Settings app from the Home display or Apps viewer
- ☒ Select Apps and move through the list of built-in and downloaded apps on your device
- ☒ Locate the Camera app, and click on it to access information of the app
- ☒ Tap Camera settings
- ☒ Locate Shooting methods on the next display and talking on it. The different

shooting methods for the Camera app will be displayed on the next display

- ☒ Locate Voice commands and switch on the toggle next to it. This will allow voice commands to be used to capture photos and shoot videos with the default Camera app

Test it out by saying the fixed commands. Speak clearly, so the device accomplishes them appropriately.

How To Use the Auto Frame for Video

This feature was first initiated on the Galaxy Fold series, and now it's finally here on the S22 series.

The Auto framing feature will automatically identify any person in the viewfinder and track anyone who enters the screen. You can make use of it on both lenses of the Galaxy S22.

☒ Select the Camera app and tap on Video

☒ Pick the Auto framing icon at the bottom right side of the screen. The icon will turn yellow once activated.

Using the auto frame for video:

☒ The auto framing icon will be highlighted in the Camera app

☒ Place your phone in a decent distance away from the subject so they can be properly captured.

☒ Pick Record to start recording

☒ When a new image enters the viewfinder, the camera will follow them while focusing on the initial subject

- Click Stop when you've finished filming.

What Is Samsung Galaxy S22 Voice Commands

By now, you would have successfully triggered the Voice commands feature. You can now use the default commands to make a photo or video. Here are the default voice commands on your device:

- Capture
- Cheese
- Smile
- Shoot
- Record a video

If it fails to work, restart your device and initiate the Camera app.

CHAPTER 16

How To Customize Camera Settings

While the default Camera app of device is adequate for taking superb pictures, you may need to tweak some camera settings for it to work the way you desire.

Your Smartphone camera settings include:

- Scene optimizes
- Scan QR codes
- Picture formats
- Shot suggestions
- Save selfies as previewed
- Swipe shutter button to
- Grid lines
- Selfie color tone
- Permissions
- Location tags

- ☒ Video stabilization
- ☒ Tracking auto-focus
- ☒ Settings to keep
- ☒ Vibration feedback
- ☒ Auto FPS
- ☒ Shooting methods
- ☒ Advanced recording options
- ☒ Reset settings

The camera settings are grouped into seven groupings on the settings page:

1. Intelligent features
2. Pictures
3. Selfies
4. Videos
5. General
6. Privacy
7. Others

To customize the Galaxy S22's camera settings, enter the Camera app and click on the Settings icon at the top left of the viewfinder, and navigate through.

Intelligent Features

1. Scene optimizer: This feature automatically sets the default camera according to the scene that was captured, thanks to Samsung's AI technology.

   The scene optimizer is usually enabled by default on your device. It also gives you access to scan document.

2. Shot suggestions: This feature assists you to get the best focus depending on the situation of the immediate scene.

While scene optimizer automatically adjusts the camera settings for you in the background, shot suggestions notifies you that the focus is good or bad. It doesn't alter any of the camera settings for you like the scene optimizer.

3. Scan QR codes: The device camera automatically recognizes QR codes and takes necessary actions.

Pictures

4. Swipe shutter button to: By default, if you double tap the shutter key on your device Camera app, it will record a video.

However, if you swipe down the shutter button to:

☒ Take burst shots

☒ Create GIFs

Note: You can only choose any of the aforementioned, according to factory settings, it is set to capture burst shots.

5. Picture formats: By default, the Galaxy S22 saves photos in JPEG format which can be viewed in most devices.

However, the issue is the compression efficiency of JPEG format is inconsiderable to the size of many other modern formats.

On your device, the default photo format is the HEIF which conserves about 30-60% of the device's storage.

6. Shooting methods: The Galaxy S22 has many shooting techniques in the Camera app. The camera's shutter

button is not the only way to capture photos on the Galaxy S22.

7. Grid lines: This feature, when enabled, divides the Galaxy S22's preview screen in the Camera app into nine equal portions. It helps you to follow the rule of the thirds.

8. Location tags: The device enables users to save the location of the photo or video even after a long period. It automatically becomes part of the metadata of that particular photo or video. You can allow it or disallow it for privacy.

Selfies

9. Save selfies as previewed

Normally, when using the fore camera, the preview screen shows a mirrored image.

On your device, you can save your selfies as mirrored photos. So, if you enable Save selfies as previewed, it means you're saving the mirrored photo that is displayed on the preview screen.

10. Selfie color tone: On your device, you can select the color brightness for your selfies; Normal (default) or bright. This color tone adjustment affects only your skin in selfies.

Video

11. Auto FPS: Once this feature is allowed, it can alter the frame rate automatically while in video style. If you need to record a video in low light, you can record a bright video by lowering the frame rate.

12. Video stabilization: This feature assists you to stabilize the video you're recording, hence avoiding unstable or blurry videos. For added stabilization, enable super-steady.

13. Advanced recording options: You can alter the advanced recording options on your device camera app settings. Here are the advanced recording options: Reduce file size, Zoom-in mic, and HDR 10+ video. Reduce file size enables you to alter the video

format of your device from MP4 format to the modern HEVC. Zoom-in mic enables you to maintain the audio when zoomed in or out of a video.

14. Tracking auto-focus: This gesture is highly beneficial for a subject motion when recording a video.

General

☒ Pick the Camera app from the home display

☒ Click on the Settings icon at the upper left of the display in the Camera app

☒ From the camera screen, swipe sideways to show the available options

☒ Click settings, and select between General and Shooting Methods.

- ☒ Enable or disable any of the options below by switching on or off their toggles
- ☒ Scene optimizer
- ☒ Scan QR codes
- ☒ Shot suggestions
- ☒ Video stabilization
- ☒ Audio HDR
- ☒ Shutter sound
- ☒ Save selfies as previewed
- ☒ Shooting methods
- ☒ Location tags
- ☒ Vibration feedback

How to Configure the Shooting Methods

- ☒ Tap the Camera app on your device

- Click on the Settings apparatus at the upper left of the preview screen

- Select Shooting methods from the Settings menu

- Select the toggle beside any of the options; Voice commands, Floating shutter button, Show palm.

CHAPTER 17

How to Create/Decorate an AR Emoji Short Video

This device comes with an incredible camera feature known as the AR Zone.

AR Zone enables users to access different AR-related properties such as AR Emoji studio,

AR Emoji Camera, AR Doodle, etc. However, some of these properties may depend on the service provider used.

The device's AR Zone enables users to use AR Emojis as their profile pictures in contacts and Samsung accounts.

Here are the different AR Zone features:

- ☒ AR Emoji Camera: Pick the Camera to produce your personal My Emoji avatar

- ☒ AR Emoji Studio: You can personalize and edit your My Emoji avatar

- ☒ AR Doodle: This feature adds lines or handwriting to the background of your video, and tracks subjects in the camera, so they change with you

☒ AR Emoji Stickers: You can include AR Emoji Stickers to your My Emoji avatar

☒ Deco Pic: Create photos or videos using the camera.

Follow the guidelines below to create/decorate an AR Emoji Short Video:

☒ Enter the Camera app on the Galaxy S22

☒ Select the AR Zone in the Camera app

☒ Tap on AR Emoji Studio

☒ Select from the options; Create a video, Lock screen, or Call screen

- Pick your desired template
- To alter the background, go to the Gallery app by clicking on the Gallery icon
- Tap Save to save the newly created video. You can view the video in the Gallery app
- To use the video at that moment, tap an option at the end of the screen.

AR Emoji Camera

- Locate the AR Zone on your device's Camera app
- Tap on AR Emoji Camera
- Select the desired emoji and mode

Note: The modes you select will be based on the emoji you select.

1. Scene: The emoji copies your current expression.

2. Mask: The emoji's face displays over your face like a mask.

3. Mirror: The emoji copies your body's movements.

4. Play: The emoji is displayed on a real background.

To capture a picture, click on the Emoji icon or long press to record a video.

You can check these photos and videos in the Gallery app.

How to Activate AR Doodle

☒ Locate AR Zone on the device's camera

☒ Tap AR Doodle. Immediately after, the camera will begin to capture the subject in front of the screen, and when it does, the recognition portion will show on the screen.

☒ Click the Brush icon to write or draw in the recognition area. Change to the rear camera to write or draw outside the recognition area. You can also record yourself doodling.

☒ Pick the Record button to record a video.

☒ Click the Stop button to stop the record. You can view this and share in the Gallery app.

Albums

The device enables you to set up similar photos into an album, so you can easily come back to them.

- ☒ From the pictures tab, long press on an image to select it. Or tap on the three vertical options to display more options, tap Edit, and select your desires photo.

- ☒ Tap More at the bottom of the screen

- ☒ Select Copy to Album to copy the image to your album or pick Move to album to cut and paste the image into another album.

- ☒ Pick the album you intend to move the album to, and the image will be saved there.

- ☒ To generate a new album, pick the Albums tab below the screen, and tap More options.

☒ Tap Create album. Input the preferred name of album, and talking Create. Move photos to the new album using the steps aforementioned.

Stories

Stories have a comparable function to albums, but with stories, you can switch your images into collages and GIFs.

You will find your story in the Stories folder in the Gallery app, though you can keep adding or removing photos.

This feature enables you to create a slideshow of your photos and videos.

☒ Enter the Gallery app and locate Stories

☒ Click on the three vertical point (More options)

☒ Tap on Create story

☒ Input the preferred name for the Story, then tap Create

☒ Select your preferred photos and videos, and click Done.

Syncing Images and Video

The Galaxy S22 enables you to trust Microsoft OneDrive app to safeguard all your valuable pictures and videos.

OneDrive enables you to automatically sync your Gallery (when set) and restore lost pictures and videos.

Note: The country and carrier determine the accessibility of this function.

☒ Download Microsoft OneDrive app and provide your Microsoft account.

☒ Pick the Gallery app and click More options (three dots) at the bottom.

☒   Tap Settings, and switch on the toggle beside Sync with OneDrive to use it.

If you've formerly signed in to your Microsoft account, but yet to sign into your Samsung account, you'll be left with just an option; Cloud sync.

If you've not logged into your Microsoft account, you will be asked to do so. Follow the displayed guidelines:

Since you have synced your Gallery with OneDrive, you can go through your photos and videos through another device, the OneDrive website, or the OneDrive app.

CHAPTER 18

Motion and Gesture

This Galaxy setting allows different motion-related activities.

To move to the Motion and Gesture settings on your Galaxy S22, follow the steps; Open the Settings app and Click Advanced Features, then Motions and Gestures.

Here are the available Motion and Gesture settings available on Galaxy S22:

Note: Click on the toggle beside the options to switch it on or off.

- ☒ Lift to wake: This feature cracks the screen on once you pick the device up

- ☒ Double tap to turn on screen: This feature turns the screen on once you click the screen twice

- ☒ Double tap to turn off screen: This feature switches off the screen once you click an empty space on the Home or Lock screen

- ☒ Keep screen on while viewing: This feature keeps the screen on in as much as you're looking at the screen

- ☒ Alert when device is picked up: Your device will vibrate after picking it up if you've just missed a call or received an SMS

- ☒ Mute with gestures: Place your hand on the screen while still on to subdue future calls and alarms

- ☒ Palm swipe to capture: Swipe the edge of your hand over half of the screen to capture the screen

- ☒ Turn One-handed Operations On/Off

How to Increase the Timer in Night Mode

The Night Mode on the Galaxy S22 now includes a countdown timer that tells you the time frame for a Night Mode picture to be captured. However, the firmness of the phone while you hold it to frame the scene will determine the time limit in the Night Mode.

The Night Mode utilizes long exposure to brighten the photo for a detailed and clearer photo in low-light conditions. By default, the device keeps the shutter open for 3 to 4 seconds when you press the shutter button. This usually comes out better when you steady the phone or place it on a tripod, if available.

When you keep the device stable, the camera app changes the exposure time depending on how steady the device is. When it recognizes no movement, the Night Mode keeps the shutter open for as 30 seconds. This results in a clearer photo and lesser noise compared to when the exposure time is 3 to 4 seconds.

How to Erase Objects from Your Photo

You can use the Object Eraser on your Galaxy S22 device to erase objects from any photo of your choice.

The Object Eraser tool removes unwanted objects from your photos and even allows you to undo the changes if you make a mistake.

- Enter the Gallery app and select the photo you wish to edit
- Click the Edit icon and select More options, then tap Object Eraser

☒ Highlight the object you intend to remove. For example, draw a shape around the object or tap the object. Tap Erase to eliminate it

You can tap Erase shadows and Erase reflections depending on what you intend to remove from the photo.

You can also erase everything at once or in multiple erases.

☒ There are options available on the Object Eraser feature such as the arrow buttons to undo or redo a change.

☒ Remove the unwanted objects and tap Done

☒ If you want to begin all over again, tap Revert, then click Revert to original

☒ To save your now edited photo, tap Save, then Save again.

Note: To retain the original photo, tap on More options, and tap Save as copy.

CHAPTER 19

How to Activate Voice Command

☒ Open the Settings app from the Home screen.

☒ Locate Apps, and tap on it

☒ Locate Camera to access the app's details

☒ Click on Camera settings to continue

☒ Pick Shooting methods on the next page

☒ Switch on the toggle beside Voice commands.

Bixby

Bixby is a virtual assistant that enables you to operate your device while doing something else. Bixby works with the apps on your phone and master services that you need to get done, then work with that.

The more you use Bixby, the better it changes to serving your wants.

Since Bixby has been infused into many features of your device, it can be used in multiple ways, reacting to what you're doing. Here are the available Bixby functions;

- ☒ Bixby Vision
- ☒ Bixby Voice
- ☒ Bixby Home
- ☒ Bixby Routines

Awakening Bixby with Your Voice

Bixby Voice doesn't require you to necessarily press a button when you intend to call it. The Bixby Voice permits you to wake it up by a simple "Hi, Bixby." You can do this once the feature has been established.

- ☒ Open Bixby by long pressing the side key depending on your device's settings
- ☒ Click the Compass icon (Discover) and the three vertical dots (More options)
- ☒ Tap Settings > Voice wake-up

- Click on the toggle beside Wake with "Hi, Bixby" to enable it

Communications Via Text

If you intend to send an important text message, but you're currently in the middle of something different, you can ask Bixby to perform it on your behalf. Call the attention of Bixby by saying "Hi Bixby„ or long pressing on the side key.

You can send a text using two approaches;

- Tell Bixby who you intend to send the text message to (for example, "Text Dad"). Tap on the Keyboard icon and input the message. Click on the Arrow icon, then Send option.

- The second method is to tell Bixby what you wish to send (for example, "Text Dad Good night." After Bixby writes the message, it shows you to review it, then you can now click Send.

Note: If you have two contacts bearing the same identity, Bixby will ask which one to text, then you select the exact contact, review the message, and tap Send.

Launch Bixby Vision

☒ Enter the Camera app and tap More.

☒ Tap Bixby Vision in the left corner at the top of the screen

☒ If it's your first-time using Bixby Vision, agree to the Terms of Service and Privacy Policy. Agree to the set permissions, and if desired, click on Add to add a shortcut to your device's home screen for easier access.

Using Bixby Vision

Here are some existing features in Bixby Vision:

1. Wine: This feature allows you to see the bottle's rating or know more about the vineyard from which it was created.

2. Translate: Automatically translate from one language to another from your screen's live preview. Click on T at the bottom right corner of the preview screen to view the extracted text. Then, tap on Translate, Copy, Select all, or Search.

3. Discover: Point your device's camera in the route of an interested subject and view related images on Pinterest.

4. Text: Copy removed text into the clipboard. You can easily translate a text or carry out a web search on a text that Bixby identifies. Bixby Vision gives you more knowledge on an image that you're trying to comprehend or a text. It can even assist you shop online.

5. Note: The existing screens, lenses, and settings of Bixby Vision may depend on the wireless service provider and software version of your device.

N. B: You can access Bixby Vision through your Camera, Gallery, and Samsung Internet.

Smart Things

SmartThings is a Samsung application that enables Galaxy S22 users regulate and monitor their home environment from their devices.

How to use:

- Open the SmartThings app on your device.
- Pick Devices.
- Click on Add device or the Plus icon.
- Select a device
- Connect to the device by following the on-screen rules.

How To Use Smart Select

Samsung's Smart Select enables you to select and crop images without capturing the entire screen. You can also use it to create GIFs, extract texts, and pin images.

Tips on how to use Smart Select on Galaxy S22:

1. Use Smart Select without the Galaxy S Pen

You can open Samsung Smart Select through two ways; From the S Pen's Air Command or through the Edge Panel.

2. Take screenshots in different shapes

The Smart Select enables you to capture screenshots in different shapes and sizes. You can clip screenshots in distinct shapes like rectangular, oval, or free shape using the Lasso tool.

3. Draw on clips

Once you've selected an area to clip using the Samsung Smart Select, click on the Pencil icon in the toolbar to draw on the selected clip. Click on the Pencil icon a second time to customize the pen shape, color, and size.

4. Auto select content

This feature automatically categorizes an important area in the image and selects it to crop. You can add or delete the selected area. You can use this feature to remove undesirable background from an image, extract a text as an image, crop extra items in an image, etc. The extracted clip is usually saved in PNG format, which means you can include it to other images.

5.Extract text

This feature enables you to extract text that appears in an image. You can also use it to extract texts from apps or websites that doesn't permit you to copy text such as YouTube comments, etc. This way, you don't need to manually write down a text from an image, but directly copy the text or address.

6. Create GIFs

This feature allows you to create GIFs of up to 15 seconds from any video playing on your Galaxy S22. You can also draw on the GIF.

7. Pin image to screen

This feature allows you to pin an image from an app or a website and paste it on the screen. The image will remain on the screen even when you open other apps, though you can change its position or minimize/maximize it. You can insert the pinned image into apps

that aid the Drag and Drop feature such as
Gmail.

CHAPTER 20

How to back up photos and video to one account

- ☒ Locate the Microsoft OneDrive app
- ☒ Sign into an existing account or create an account
- ☒ Link it to your Camera app and Gallery app
- ☒ Once it has identified the folders on your Galaxy S22, tap on Photos
- ☒ Activate the auto backup of your photos or videos
- ☒ Confirm that you confirm the synchronization on the account
- ☒ The backup will be activated, and you can now find all your images on your OneDrive.

Restoring Data

☒ Open the Settings app, and Click
Accounts and backup

☒ Tap Restore data

☒ If you've used the same account to
back up multiple Samsung devices, all
the backups will be shown. Select the
backup that you intend to restore.

☒ Select the apps that you intend to
restore

☒ Click on Restore

☒ If prompted, tap on Install to restore
your home screen and Apps screen.

How To Reset Camera Settings

You can restore the Galaxy S22 camera
settings, but this will not reset the Camera

app, instead it will reset the app settings by the app itself. It is more like a soft reset.

Most times, you will see that the soft reset might not do the work you desire, so you may end up opting for the hard reset. Hard resetting app implies that you will be wiping all your camera app data, but will not erase your photos.

Follow the guidelines below to reset your Camera settings:

- ☒ Go to the Settings app and tap on Apps to access the application manager.

- ☒ Open the Camera app on the Apps page.

- ☒ Click on the Camera app to access information on the app.

- ☒ Scroll down and locate the Storage entry for the Camera app.

You can also access the Camera app information page from the home screen or Apps screen by long pressing on the Camera app icon. Tap on the I icon to open the Camera app information page.

⊠ On the Storage information page for the Camera app, pick one of the two options; Clear cache or Clear data.

The Clear cache option will not affect your Galaxy S22 camera settings, but will clean out some unwanted files associated with the Camera App. Doing this will help solve some weird camera issues.

The Clear data option is like a factory data reset for the Camera app, clearing out any user-generated data on the

Camera app. It will go back to the Camera app to its "factory" state.

☒ After clicking on Clear data, a confirmation pop-up will appear.

Director's View Mode on Galaxy S22

The Director's view mode is one of the innovative features that was introduced in the Galaxy S21.

The Galaxy S22 Director's view mode lets you to record videos from different angles simultaneously by switching cameras.

You can view each camera's scenes through thumbnails and change the scene by selecting the thumbnails whilst recording a video.

Tips and Tricks to Improve Photography in Galaxy S22

1. Turn on the 108MP mode

The 108MP camera can be seen on the Galaxy S22, and Samsung did not enable the feature by default, so you will need to do that manually. The photos captured using this mode occupy a lot of space, so don't forget to return to the original mode after use.

2. Enable scene optimizer

When you enable this camera mode, it automatically improves your photo using AI.

This can make astonishing Instagram-worthy photos without too much effort.

The Camera app must be in Photo mode to enable it.

3. Turn on auto frame for videos

The auto frame helps you to find the suitable frame for your videos. The feature

147

automatically adjusts the zoom to put all your subjects inside the frame.

Note: You cannot use Super Steady mode after enabling Auto Frame.

4. Capture 8K snap

While in Video mode, tap on the FHD-icon at the top of the screen, and the camera will record your video in 8K.

5. Increase the timer in night mode

The Galaxy S22 night mode analyzes the screen in front by default, and fine-tunes the camera's shutter speed to suit the scene.

6. Try a different kind of portrait

Portraits on the Galaxy S22 look amazing. While the background already has the right aggregate of blur and color, you can change the background effect for a better outlook. Try different effects from Black and White to Color Point.

CONCLUSION

By now, I believe you are acquainted with the basic features and components of the Samsung Galaxy S22 from managing files to seamlessly syncing folders. After going through this manual, you would marvel at the level of interesting and up-to-date arrays of services at the tip of your fingers with the latest S22.

You can get more advance than what's presented in this particular booklet though, and make your life significantly easier with your device by downloading and installing the necessary Apps to meet your mobile needs. The processing ability of the S22 fundamentally implies to better overall user experience, smoother mobile gameplay, sustained and consistent multitasking ability, stable average to above-average uses, and better and faster processing rates for images and videos. This device has also been equipped with 4G LTE and the recently launched 5G cellular technologies, as well as support for near-field communication.

Another great feature about the Samsung Galaxy S22 is its compact relativeness compared to the previous version as well as other Android smartphones. Though the 6.1-inch screen might not serve individuals who need larger display panels for mobile video gaming but ideal for average users as the screen is similar to that of the iPhone 13.

Bear in mind that there are varieties of refreshing and cool colors to select from as the Samsung Galaxy S22, ranges in five different arrays of colors: Phantom Black, Phantom White, Green, Pink Gold or Bora Purple.

Printed in Great Britain
by Amazon

43721573R00086